How to Start a Business
In
10 days

By

K. Moni

How to Start a Business in 10 Days

This book is dedicated to my mother, Earnestine H. Williams, who supported me throughout the 61 years she was upon this earth. She was a loving, God-fearing woman which went above and beyond to raise her three children and support our father, her husband. Mother, I love you, and this one is for you.

This book is a guide to potential entrepreneurs to start a successful business in 10 days.

- If you are SERIOUS about business, this book is for you.
- If you have set aside a lump sum of MONEY, this book is for you.
- If you are NOT AFRAID of people, this book is for you.
- If you are WILLING to spend money to make money, this book is for you.
- If you want to be the BOSS, this book is for you.

"How to Start a Business in 10 days" will teach key principles in starting a successful company. It will show you ways that can help you avoid pitfalls of start-up companies. Today, many people start businesses but they do not have the money to continue the business. This book will give examples of ways to establish a firm foundation to keep steady cash flow. It will re-develop your business every year from start-up. If you are looking for the resources to grow your business, continue to read this book and you will find the answer you need. Let's get started.......

Table of Contents

Day 1: *Are you ready?*...5

Day 2: *Write It Down*...6

Day 3: *Business Plan*...7

Day 4: *Marketing Plan*..8

Day 5: *The Basics of Business*..9

Day 6: *Do your Research*..10

Day 7: *Hear and Do*..11

Day 8: *Decisions, Decisions, Decisions*..13

Day 9: *Start, Begin, Again*...14

Day 10: *Business Operations*..16

Conclusion: *Recap of Starting a Business*......................................18

Bonus: *Independent Consultants*..20

How to Start a Business in 10 Days

Day 1: *Are you ready?*

"Are you ready?" I asked this question because the business starts with you. You are the first employee of the company. You are the one that the business must please. You are the person that must be attracted to the business. Ask yourself, "Are you ready?" If you answered "yes" to this question, let's get started! You must be the cheerleader, motivator, manager, inspirational speaker and leader of the one employee that you began with which is you. A lot of people have the idea of starting a business and many will take action and start a business. However, there are only a few that will get pass the Grim Reaper of business. You can do business. You can start a business. You can be successful in business. You can make money in business. You can develop and grow your business. You can become a successful business owner. You must ask the question: Are you ready? Define success to you. Success to some people is making a lump sum of money. Success to some people is having a good marriage, good family and good job. Whatever success is to you in your personal life will be the same way you define success in your business. If you look at success in your personal life as making a lump sum of money, well by far success in your business will be defined to you as making a lump sum of money. But, ask yourself "what do you want?" Work towards the goal of what do you want. Remember, you are the first employee of your business. There are things that you have experienced whether it was good or bad on your jobs or in your trade that you would like to use or not use inside of your business. These things you need to write it down and implement. In the next chapter, we will discuss writing things down followed by implementation.

How to Start a Business in 10 Days

Day 2: *Write It Down*

Now that you have answered the following questions:

    1.) Are you ready?

    2.) What is Success to you?

    3.) What do YOU want?

It is time to WRITE IT DOWN. Yes, write down your ideas. When you write things down it looks better on paper. Therefore, you will need to develop a plan. In order to start a successful business, you will need to have a business plan, marketing plan, company name, logo, vision statement, mission statement, motto, etc. If you write down your ideas, all of these things will come to you easily. Writing ideas down the company will start to make sense to you. You will develop a vision and your imagination will take you to places that you never would have thought before. The company will become reality to you. You do not want to jump into the business too fast unprepared, but you definitely do not want to have the vision stuck in your head without implementing it. A moderate speed of implementation will take you on a successful journey.

    Writing down your ideas will also lead you on a path where you may begin with one business idea but may end up creating a totally different business. It may also lead you to several other business ideas that you will be able to grow your business. You do need a place to start your business. Well, writing down your ideas will identify how you could get started, where you could start your business, how much space you will need, how many people you will need to employ or could you start with just one person, you.

How to Start a Business in 10 Days

Day 3: *Business Plan*

As an entrepreneur, it is very important for you to write the vision and make it plain, so that if anyone decides to read it they can run with it and implement it. The Business Plan is a roadmap of your business. It is the blueprint of your business. Writing a successful business plan requires time. On Day 2, you wrote down all of your ideas. Therefore, you should be able to write out your business plan easily. What do you need in your business plan? Can you have someone else write your business plan? In this Chapter, you will be able to receive the answers to these questions. Remember, you are the one to please. You are the one employee in the beginning. You are the salesperson, manager and internal customer.

A business plan requires the following basic items:

- Executive Summary
- Keys to Success
- Mission
- Objectives
- Organization Summary
- Start-up Summary
- Services
- Market Analysis Summary
- Market Segmentation
- Target Market Segment Strategy
- Strategy and Implementation Strategy
- Competitive Edge
- Management Summary
- Personnel Plan
- Financial Plan
- Break-Even Analysis

You can look on the internet to find examples of the particular type of business that you are starting to see ways of writing your business plan. You may also have someone write your business plan for you. There are many ways to get your business plan written.

Day 4: *Marketing Plan*

Now, that you have started on your business plan or got it done. You will need to write a Marketing Plan. A lot of businesses fail because they do not know how to market their business. You have started the company but how are you going to make sales and grow your business. There are ways to advertise your business that make it appeasing to customers. Customers would like to be drawn to your company. Besides, customers are what you are interested in gaining. The more customers you gather, the more money you will make.

A marketing plan is a comprehensive blueprint which outlines an organization's overall marketing efforts. The items required in a marketing plan are the following:

- Executive Summary
- Situation Analysis
- Market Summary
- Market Analysis
- Market Needs
- Market Trends
- Market Growth
- SWOT Analysis
- Competition
- Services Offered
- Service Business Analysis
- Keys to Success
- Critical Issues
- Marketing Strategy
- Mission
- Marketing Objectives
- Financial Objectives
- Target Markets
- Positioning
- Marketing Mix
- Marketing Research
- Sales and Expense Forecast
- Marketing Expense Budget
- Contingency Plan

How to Start a Business in 10 Days

Day 5: *The Basics of Business*

Now that you have started on your Business Plan and Marketing Plan, it is time to address the basics of business. What is your vision? Every business and business owner should have a vision. As the business owner, you have a vision of the business. The business should have a vision statement. Define what you expect within the Vision Statement. Make sure to post this statement on your website and within your place of business. Remind yourself of the vision daily. This is the reason why you got started. At the beginning, you are the one employee that must be convinced of this business being a success.

Your next step is to write the Mission Statement. The mission statement is another item that needs to be posted on your website and in on the wall of your business. The mission statement is a formal summary of the aims and values of a company, organization or individual. It will also be included in the Business Plan and/or Marketing Plan for your business.

After you have established your vision and mission statements, you should define the goal of your company. What would you like the company to accomplish? This goal should be reached on a measurable basis. If you were to evaluate whether or not this goal was met on a daily, weekly, monthly or yearly basis. An example of a goal is to provide excellent customer service. This example can be measured daily, weekly, monthly or even yearly.

Every company needs to have values. You have values in your every day life. These are some of the values you should implement for your company.

Day 6: *Do your Research*

Starting a business requires research. You need to study the market that you are entering. Ask questions. Do the leg work. What do you as an internal customer want? What do your external customers want? You have to know what type of business you want. Do you want a large or small business? Do you want a cradle to grave business or an online store? What will sell quick or what will take time to sell? Do you want to offer services or a product? Do you have enough experience to enter into that market? Do you need to go back to school in order to learn a trade or do you need to hire someone to offer that expertise?

Starting a business can be easy. Maintaining the busy is the hard part. You have the money to start the business but do you have the money to maintain the business. Most businesses require you to spend money in order to make money. You can not be afraid of people and definitely can not be afraid of losing. Most entrepreneurs will tell of you of their success stories, but will not share with you the many failures they experienced before hitting it BIG. Do not be afraid to ask for help. Look for a mentor in business. You may not necessarily need a physical person to assist you along the way. You can read books and go to seminars in order to learn about a situation you need help with. Your answer could be hidden in a book. That is the reason why this book along with a couple of my other books has been written to help people like you. It gives answers to how to start and maintain a successful business. These are the basic things you need to know and if you hear and do, your business will succeed.

How to Start a Business in 10 Days

Day 7: *Hear and Do*

Okay, okay, okay....Way to go. You have made it to Day 7. This is the day you have been waiting for. Time to go for it! You have had time to think about it, talk yourself out of it or decide to move forward. Now, it's time to locate an attorney, banker and accountant. These are the three (3) most important people in your business life. You will call them family. The relationship you will establish with them must be a relationship of family. They are a part of your business and will play a major part in your business life. After you done your research on who you would like to be your attorney, banker and accountant, you will need to start scheduling a meeting with your attorney. Next, schedule an appointment with your accountant. The last person you will meet with to establish your family is your banker.

At the meeting with your attorney, take your business plan, marketing plan and checkbook. The attorney will take you serious and know that you are serious about business when you have your ducks in a row. He or she sees that you have your marketing and business plan. They will know that you have an idea of what you want and the plan of how you are going to go about getting it. The attorney will ask you what type of business you would like to have such as a Partnership, LLC, Corporation, etc... When you wrote your business plan it should have helped you decide which type of business works best for you. Some attorneys require their fee upfront and provide these fees at the consultation. The attorney will take care of the Articles of Incorporation and if you need a Federal Id no. some will go the extra mile in setting this help for you. The Banker will need the certified copy of the Articles of Incorporation to establish a Co.

Bank Acct. The accountant will help you decide if you have chosen the right entity such as LLC or Corporation that will work financially best for you. They will also help you with your financial statements in case you may need to request a loan.

Day 8: *Decisions, Decisions, Decisions*

As CEO of your business, you will have to make decisions. You can not be afraid of making choices. The problem is making the right choice. Every day you make decisions whether good or bad. In business, you must learn to make right decisions. It will help you in the long run. In order to make the right choice, evaluate the situation from all angles. Do not make a decision in a short time frame, especially if you are not the only employee. The decision you make affects your entire team. People would like to be on a winning team. If they notice their boss make good decisions, they will be loyal to you. However, if you choose not to make a decision than your employees, clients and customers may not take you seriously. They will get frustrated and would like to go to a place where decisions are made efficiently. There is a saying that states, "Be decisive. Right or wrong, make a decision. The road of life is paved with flat squirrels who couldn't make a decision."

Not only is it important for CEOs to make a decision, but it is vital for the management team that the CEO appoints are able to make timely decisions. Your company will only be as strong as the people who you hire. Having a management team that is not decisive can negatively affect your company. As a CEO, you would not know everything that your employees would know. It is good to have an overall understanding of what the job entails. The staff you hire should be experts in their fields and can help you run the company successfully. Release the pressure that you should know it all. However, you should know enough to make decisions and improvements to your company.

How to Start a Business in 10 Days

Day 9: *Start, Begin, Again*

Now that you know that decisions are important, you should decide when to start your business. If you need to quit a job in order to begin, you should be prepared with at least three (3) months of income for your personal spending as well as six (6) months of sustaining income for your business. Or less you are starting a daycare there is no guarantee that you will make a profit within the first couple of months. That is why it is smart to have funds available to uphold your family and your business. You may have heard of people quitting their jobs and starting a business with only a small amount of money. That is far and between and not my recommendation for you. I would like for you to be wise. You can work yourself out of the job that you are on to help start your business. You should meet with your accountant, banker and attorney before quitting your job. Get everything done while working. Do not work on your business while working at your job. You need to get use to working over 40 hours per work and this is a quick way to practice doing just that. Besides you do not want to reap negativity within your company. Treat the job like your business and what you would like your employees to do while working at your company. How would you like it if, your employees stole supplies while working on starting a business at your company? The feeling would not be satisfactory.

What if you decide to work a job while starting your business? Until your business has enough funds to bring you off the job, it is perfectly fine. Some people jump out immediately off a job and do not succeed in having sufficient income to maintain the business and living expenses for their family. They normally have to go back and start again at getting a job to help financially. You are doing the opposite way. Staying on a job and running a company works in a positive or negative way but both can lead to a profit. The negative way can also lead to a loss that will end your business. If you are not a self-sufficient company that makes you money while sleeping, the company may suffer. You need to put in the time and effort to grow your company. For example, if you have a restaurant while working on a job for another company, you may be losing money by employees taking food while you are not there and treating customers badly plus the quality of the food may not be up to your standards. If this is the case, you may need to think about changing the restaurant opening hours. It is perfectly fine to have a restaurant open only on the weekends or just breakfast hours or dinner hours. This will create an atmosphere that reserves your quality, excellent customer service, profits and brand.

    I would suggest knowing when to quit your job. There are entrepreneurs who are working a job while running their business and are losing money. They could be making more money in business than working both job and business. But, they are too afraid to jump. How do you know when to quit your job? You know when your brand is well-known. Customers are seeking you out and the demand of your product is at an all time high. Let me tell you something. There are a high percentage of businesses that fail within the first year and most successful entrepreneur had several failures before getting it right. But, your business is booming and your potential customers need you to quit your job. Your customers are pulling you to greatness. Stop being afraid and just do it. You will not fail.

How to Start a Business in 10 Days

Day 10: *Business Operations*

Your company business plan and marketing plan are in place. They are the footprints of your company. You have hired an attorney, accountant, and banker. Hopefully, you formed a relationship with them because they are your family now and for the next many years that you are in business. You have an understanding of making decisions. Therefore, you have decided on a location of where you would like to operate your business. Location is important for your business. In your research, you should have checked out the geographical location that is best for your company. For example, if you are operating a thrift store, please do not have it in a rich neighborhood. It should be located in an area that low-income families could walk to your store and purchase your products.

You have decided on when to start your business. Should you have a grand opening if you have a store front business? Yes. You should introduce potential customers to what you will have to offer. Present your offers to them in a way that keep them wanting more of your product or services. Having a launch party, can help make an introduction of your company.

Invite the community to get the word out. In the beginning, most of your business will come by word of mouth. Therefore, make a good first impression so that the customers will continue to want to come back.

Hiring the appropriate staff and the right amount of people for your business is important as well. You do not need to be overstaffed nor understaffed. You do need to have well-trained employees. A lot of successful entrepreneurs do not recommend hiring family and close friends especially for your first business. Use your digression on who can represent you and your company in a positive way. Hire someone who can adjust to your standards and demonstrates your company values to the public.

Conclusion: *Recap of Starting a Business*

Step 1: Decide on a business.

Start a business that you are passionate about and can do it without thinking about it. Meaning it is your God-given gift and talent.

Step 2: Create your business plan.

If you unable to create a business plan on your own, hire a company to do it for you. The business plan will serve as a blueprint for your company to run successfully. You will need it to take your attorney, accountant and banker.

Step 3: Create your marketing plan.

A marketing plan will help reinvent your company when you think that sales are down. It is vital to have this in place before starting your business. You should have it ready before you meet with your attorney, accountant and banker.

Step 4: Choose an Attorney.

Choosing the right attorney for your business will be significant. You should do your research on a potential attorney. You can visit www.avvo.com to find ratings on the attorney you select. You do not have to choose the first attorney that you meet with. You are interviewing them as well and they must believe in your vision and your company. Please choose an attorney that show interest in you and your vision. They may have to fight for you in court. Choose wisely.

Step 5: Choose an Accountant.

Select an accountant that understands your business and represent other business clients like yours. You can search the internet for an accountant in your local area. The accountant should be trustworthy since they are dealing with your financial records. Choose wisely.

Step 6: Choose a Bank for your business.

Select a bank that has FDIC and excellent customer service. If you operating on the weekend, you may want to select a bank that has weekend service. Make sure there is a banker on site that you can relate to and form a business relationship with. Having a banker when you run into overdraft problems can help your business significantly.

How to Start a Business in 10 Days

Step 7: Choose a Location.

As stated earlier, choose a location that your customers are in high demand for your services or products. Placing your company in a demanding area is crucial. Startups do extremely well when the place of their business is in a good location. Pay attention to the demographics.

Step 8: Hire Staff.

Recruiting the right staff can be critical for the success of the company. Hire employees that represent the company values and who are highly skilled in their profession. After you hire them, continue to train them on the company policies and procedures.

Step 9: Start your business.

You can begin now. Following Steps 1 through 8, you are guaranteed to be on the right path to having a successful business. Good luck! Remember, you can do this!

Bonus: *Independent Consultants*

After working for yourself, it is kind of hard working for someone else. With Independent consulting, you must have a large clientele database. You can land one major contract. However, you must network with the right people and have the right connections. My recommendations for if you would like to become an Independent Consultant, is to join local community organizations such as the Better Business Bureau, Leadership organizations, etc… You should make people aware of who you are. This is an important way of building your brand. What do you stand for? You are the business. Therefore, have a motto for yourself. My dad is a retired insurance sales agent for a large life insurance agency. He had a motto for himself and it was "I'm W.L. here to sale and service you well." It was a catchy phrase for his clientele. He was the Top agent at his company winning several awards including Agent of the Year. Customers were seeking him out and wanted to sign up with him. He was well-known in the community. He could have been Mayor if he ran for office. Speaking of the Mayor, they became friends. The mayor knew my dad had great influence in the community. Boy, was he right. Let's just say, he remained in office until after my dad retired and relocated to the same city as myself and my siblings.

Who you know is vitally important. Sometimes by whom you know can be an avenue of how you get a job. This can be the same way to get in the door to becoming an independent consultant. It is really easy to do. Simple is better. Not making things difficult can get you where you would like to be.

A friend of a friend will get you where you need to be as well. Enlarging your circle and being with friends such as people who are like-minded. Some people cannot see the vision of your brand the way you envision it. Therefore, you need to be around someone who is on your professional level and above, if they allow you to join them. I'm not saying not to be around people who are below your professional level. You can but sharing the vision of your brand should be off limits.

As an Independent Contractor, landing that one major contract can make all the difference. You may ask how do I get that contract or any contract. There are several ways but the main one is becoming a subcontractor to a large or small business. So, how do I get in with the large or small business? One way is becoming a member of the Chamber of Commerce in your area. If you attended a major university that performs government contracting services, register with their career services department. Allow the Director of the Career Development Services Department to become aware of who you are and learn your name. You should be on a first name basis with the Director. Universities and Colleges typically love supporting their Alumni's and are willing to support you more than regular businesses. They may connect you with another Graduate who is in the same industry at the least.

Attending Industry Day in your local community is another way to enter into the market. Becoming an active member of an association in your field study will also open doors for you. Attending different Leadership events will be a quick way to market your brand. The key point of entering the market is to build your brand allowing it to represent who you are, selling yourself and bring awareness to who you are as an independent contractor. Remember, it is easy to enter into the market. Once you get in make sure your brand represents who you are as a person and awareness to your company.

About the Author

K. Moni is an entrepreneur who has owned several companies including an accountant firm, investment firm, government contracting company and a daycare. K. Moni is currently pursuing a doctorate degree in Strategy and Innovation. K. Moni background consists of a Bachelor of Science degree in Accounting, a Master's degree in Management, over thirteen (13) years of Accounting experience and over nine (9) years of government contracting experience. K. Moni is actively involved in community and national leadership programs. K. Moni's goal is to help inspiring entrepreneurs accomplish successful operating businesses that last longer than statistics odds. K. Moni provides tools and methods that entrepreneurs can use to change their way of evaluating their companies to bring about profits and sustaining growth.

How to Start a Business in 10 Days

Other Books by the Author:

How to Run a Successful Business (publishing soon)

How to Market your Business (publishing soon)

How to Make Money for your Business (publishing soon)

www.ingramcontent.com/pod-product-compliance
Lightning Source LLC
Chambersburg PA
CBHW070721210526
45170CB00021B/1395